WARRINGTON
THROUGH TIME
Janice Hayes

AMBERLEY

Market Gate looking down Bridge Street in the 1900s.

First published 2010

Amberley Publishing Plc
Cirencester Road, Chalford,
Stroud, Gloucestershire, GL6 8PE

www.amberley-books.com

Copyright © Janice Hayes &
Warrington Borough Council, 2010

The right of Janice Hayes & Warrington Borough
Council to be identified as the Authors of this
work has been asserted in accordance with the
Copyrights, Designs and Patents Act 1988.

ISBN 978 1 84868 564 2

British Library Cataloguing in Publication Data.
A catalogue record for this book is available from
the British Library.

Typeset in 9.5pt on 12pt Celeste.
Typesetting by Amberley Publishing.
Printed in the UK.

Introduction

"Warrington as we find it today is an enterprising and progressive town... with unlimited scope for development. The town has altered considerably during the last few decades, and the narrow winding main streets have gradually given place to broad and dignified thoroughfares. Formerly it was a picturesque old-world place....but the town still possesses many places of great antiquity." This extract from *The Warrington Guardian's Directory and History of Warrington and its Environs* may have been written in 1908 but it also chronicles similar changes witnessed by present day Warringtonians in a post industrial landscape.

Undoubtedly Warrington has changed considerably in the century and a half since the infancy of photography in the 1850s. Many of these changes were also witnessed in towns and cities across the country; others were the result of planned local development such as the 1968 Master Plan for Warrington New Town.

As the era of the horseless carriage gave way to the age of the motor Warrington felt a particular impact because of its strategic importance as a vital node on the national transport network. Although nearby motorways siphoned off some of the through traffic the rise in local commuter traffic and family car journeys inevitably placed a strain on the local infrastructure. Whole areas of the town were transformed by the creation of ring roads and distributor roads designed to relieve traffic congestion. Although streetscapes seemed dominated by a plethora of essential road signage the town centre was enhanced by public art.

Traditional family run businesses like butchers, grocers and corner shops disappeared to be replaced by the chain stores and supermarkets to be found nationwide. Warringtonians noticed these changes even more vividly because of the planned redevelopment of the town centre in the early 1900s and then with the later twentieth century regeneration of the Old Market Area, the creation of Golden Square

"Come on the Wire" was the cry on the rugby ground but it was firms like Rylands which helped to make the town prosperous.

and out of town retail parks. These created a new focus for the new leisure activity of shopping.

The nationwide decline in heavy industries saw Warrington cease to be a *"Town of Many Industries"* where the majority of the workforce toiled in factories but instead prosper in an era of the service economy and in the technology led environment of the new business parks.

The geography of Warrington also changed with the local government reform of 1974 which brought parts of old Lancashire and Cheshire within the borough boundaries. Some traditional villages like Grappenhall, Thelwall and Appleton outwardly retained their rural character whilst new districts at Padgate; Birchwood, Westbrook and Chapelford emerged from previously derelict areas of the Second World War installations. The population of the town also swelled and by the early twenty-first century included new residents from the contemporary global society.

Warringtonians past and present have given the town its unique character and many of them look out at us curiously from the official photographs, picture postcards and informal snapshots as if to help us understand how their town has changed through time.

CHAPTER 1

Bridge Foot

Warrington Bridge remains a crucial crossing point over the Mersey

"Warrington is one of the principal thoroughfares of the north, being the only entrance to from the south to all the north-west part of England," wrote Aiken in 1795. By the thirteenth century a bridge had replaced the old ford at Latchford. The fine three arched stone Victoria Bridge was replaced by the present bridge between 1911-1915. Today only a capstone of the old bridge remains at Bridge Foot.

Traffic congestion at Bridge Foot!

The twenty foot wide Victoria Bridge, opened in 1837, the year of Queen Victoria accession, was already proving a bottleneck by the end of her reign. Fortunately for today's weary motorists it was replaced by a much wider single span reinforced concrete bridge, designed by local engineer John James Webster. The early twentieth century visionaries behind the scheme could not have foreseen the vast increase in road traffic the new bridge would have to withstand.

Aerial views of Bridge Foot; 1970s and early twenty-first century

Despite the motorway network siphoning off much through traffic from the town by the late twentieth century the growth of local commuter traffic led to the building of an additional crossing at Bridge Foot in the 1990s (seen below) and wider traffic lanes.

War and peace at Warrington Bridge

In August 1904 General Booth's motor car tour from Lands End to Aberdeen crossed Warrington Bridge where the crowd *"gave an enthusiastic expression of the work of this veteran founder of the Salvation Army."* Fittingly his car displayed a banner proclaiming *"blood and fire!"* Today he would have seen a surprisingly tranquil scene from his car window as nature makes a welcome return to the waterside amidst the traffic noise.

From Bishops Wharf to Riverside retail park

By the nineteenth century the river was also a major transport highway serving the town's industries. Although most activity was concentrated at Bank Quay a second dock developed at Bishop's Wharf serving mainly local tanneries and paper mills. By the late 1950s (seen below) many of the tanneries had closed and the river boats soon disappeared. By the early twenty-first century a new retail park replaced the old warehouses.

Knutsford Road and Wilderspool Causeway 1900s and 2010

The approaches to Warrington Bridge were also been remodelled over the last century as traffic volume increased. The junction of Knutsford Road and Wilderspool Causeway was widened in the early 1900s and later in the mid 1950s. Long before the days of MP3 players this purveyor of "*gramophones and phonographs*" (above) was forced to advertise a closing down sale prior to demolition. The days of the Norton Arms (far right) were also numbered.

Rush hour at Wilderspool!

Whilst the sight of a steam train travelling on the Warrington to Altrincham line via Arpley Station was an irresistible lure for Edwardian children the constant closing of the railway crossing gates had created a major traffic bottleneck by the mid twentieth century. A solution arrived with the opening of an elevated road crossing opened on 16 May 1957. Not long afterwards the railway it was designed to cross fell victim to Dr Beeching's axe!

Warrington Academy moves with the times

A major obstacle to road widening at Bridge Foot was the historic Warrington Academy where Joseph Priestley had been a tutor. Demolition was avoided by a remarkable feat of engineering on 22 May 1981 when Pynford's winched the old building to an adjacent vacant spot after slicing it from its foundations. The road was widened and the Academy substantially remodelled to emerge as the new headquarters of the Warrington Guardian newspaper.

The changing face of Mersey Street 1970s and 2009

As part of the new traffic circulation system at Bridge Foot narrow winding Mersey Street also needed to be widened. This meant curtains for J. Leigh and Sons who had supplied furnishings and ladies', gents' and children's clothes since 1846.

CHAPTER 2

Bridge Street

Bridge Street: the artery to Warrington's town centre

Travellers crossing Warrington Bridge were funnelled down Bridge Street to the town centre. In the thirteenth century the Boteler family had built the bridge as a route to their lucrative market and with it a *"New Street"* later appropriately known as Bridge Street. The early 1900s view (above) shows the winding route to Market Gate and the distinctive tower building which was demolished to make way for the old Academy.

What a circus in Lower Bridge Street!

It's hard to imagine in today's relatively traffic-free zone that in the 1830s about sixty stage coaches a day incessantly careered along Bridge Street to major coaching inns like the Red Lion. Even as late as the 1960s (inset) this was still a major traffic route. As for the elephants lumbering through in the 1920s they were probably on their way to a seasonal show in Victoria Park!

Academy Way divides Bridge Street

Walking Day photographs help to show the changing face of Bridge Street. In 1906 these decorated floats passed by the arched entrance to Rose and Crown Street where petrol for the new-fangled horseless carriages could be bought. Eighty years later the motor car caused the demolition of these same buildings as a new inner ring road called Academy Way was built to join up with existing Friars Gate.

Changing Bridge Street 1900s and early twenty-first century

Upper Bridge Street has changed considerably since the 1900s. The earlier photograph dating from 1904 (looking towards Market Gate) shows the emergence of today's familiar shop fronts built behind the line of the old narrow street. Workmen are busy extending the existing Rylands Street to Latchford tramline to Stockton Heath to be opened in July 1905. In the mid 1990s another team of workmen were hard at work creating a memorial to those killed and injured by the explosion of an IRA bomb in Bridge Street on 20 March 1993. Unveiled in 1996 and inspired by the Book of Revelation, the sculpture is known as the River of Life. It was created by sculptor Steven Broadbent with a central water feature linked to twelve plaques created by local schools representing *"the leaves of the tree for the healing of nations"*

Spot the difference in Upper Bridge Street?

A century separates these two views and at first glance little has changed. Today the trees accompanying the River of Life partially obscure the view towards Market Gate from the junction with Rylands Street. In the earlier view (above) dating from about 1910 the buildings in distant Horsemarket Street and Sankey Street still await twentieth century modernisation.

Bridge Street viewed from Market Gate 1900s and 2009

As the 1910 Walking Day procession nears Market Gate the widening of the West Side of Bridge Street (on the right of these pictures) was complete. Parts of the East Side were also rebuilt before the First World War. Today the cobblestones have returned whilst the decorative shields high on the lampposts celebrate past Lords of the Manor of Warrington and local landowners.

Bustling Bridge Street

The earlier photograph shows a Saturday afternoon rush hour at 5.20 pm in 1935. The majority of the pedestrians are rugby fans streaming back into town from the match at the old Wire's Stadium at Wilderspool. Last minute shoppers would need to fight their way into department stores such as Hodgkinson's and Lee and Clarke's as Bridge Street was still the main shopping destination. Today's crowds are probably heading for Golden Square.

Marking the passage of time in Bridge Street

In 1908 the last premises on the corner of Bridge Street and Sankey Street were facing demolition to be replaced by the first phase of a proposed *"spacious circus, perfectly symmetrical in shape with a ring of singularly graceful buildings."* Only this corner was built to the original design and for many generations of Warringtonians came to be known as Boots Corner.

Bridge Street meets the town centre at Market Gate 1960 and 2009

Travellers reaching the town centre end of Bridge Street would find themselves at a crossroads where the main north-south and east-west road routes met. Facing them was Horsemarket Street with Sankey Street to the left and Buttermarket Street to the right while the crossroads came to be known as Market Gate (the street leading to the market.) How formal the 1960s shoppers look with overcoats and hats!

CHAPTER 3
A Market Town

The Old Market Area 1900s and 1970s

Warrington's market dates back to at least 1277 and by the eighteenth century had moved off the main crossroad into The Old Market Place. The 1900s view (above) shows the open Fish Market where Mr Lee is selling oysters. The later picture shows the Old Market Place in the early 1970s. Many of the buildings on the left dated from the 1850s and were replicated during the construction of Golden Square.

Time passes by the Barley Mow

The Barley Mow is the oldest building in the town centre dating from the time of Queen Elizabeth I in the later sixteenth century. Note the subtle changes in its appearance from the 1900s picture above to the mid 1970s photograph below. The building on its left was formerly the offices of William Beamont, Warrington's first mayor, but was better known as the Readicut wool shop by the time of the later photograph!

Golden Square 2010 and early 1970s

Those enjoying the café culture of today's Golden Square would find this early 1970s view towards Market Gate almost unrecognisable but a closer look reveals the shops of Horsemarket Street in the background down Cheapside. On the left is the imposing Italian style Market Hall opened in 1856 and designed by Mr Stevens as part of an earlier remodelling of the Old Market Place.

A view towards Sankey Street from the Barley Mow 1968 and 2009

The Old Market area was linked to Sankey Street by a narrow entry, officially called Castle Street but popularly known as "The Cock and Trumpet" entry (seen behind the parked van). The Blackburne Arms pub in the background was named after the Blackburne family of Orford Hall, who as Lords of the Manor of Warrington had owned the market area until the redevelopment of the mid 1850s.

Building Golden Square 1980s and early twenty-first century

Today's Golden Square was created by construction work on an epic scale. The 1970s-80s phase swept away all but the Barley Mow and the Old Fish Market, creating an open piazza with shopping malls and replica Victorian buildings. The second phase built 2004-7 replaced the bus station and Legh Street multi storey car park (seen right on the bottom view) creating a 365,000 square foot extension of prime retail space.

No more plaice in the Old Market Place!

1970s shoppers (above) stroll through the Old Fish Market which was originally an open shed adjoining the Market Hall. By the 1970s the graceful structure was obscured by ugly side panelling which protected traders and customers from the weather. Now restored to its former glory as the focal point of the Old Market Place it houses a variety of entertainments and festivals instead of fishmongers, cheese stalls and tripe sellers.

From rationing to retail therapy

In the post-war austerity of the 1950s there was little to buy in the general market to be found behind the Barley Mow. Shoppers used to the restraints of rationing bought essentials from sparsely stocked fold-up stalls. The brightly lit shopping malls of Golden Square were born of a different era at the dawn of the twenty-first century when consumers shopped for pleasure before a credit-crunch brought renewed austerity.

The changing face of Bank Street

In preparation for the building of the first phase of Golden Square the market was relocated to Bank Street in 1974 forming the core of the South East quadrant of the new town centre. The 1900s photograph (below) reveals an area of densely packed housing created in the 1840s-60s for migrant workers, many of Irish origin. Slum clearance of the 1930s brought new homes in the suburbs and a development opportunity.

Time flies in Times Square early 1980s and 2010

With the completion of the Academy Way section of the inner ring road attention turned to the development of a new pedestrian shopping precinct next to the new market. By 1986 Massey & Garnett's distinctive Times Square had replaced the shabby premises of the discount carpet warehouse pictured above.

CHAPTER 4
Sankey Street

Sankey Street viewed from Market Gate 1926 and 2009

First appearing as *Sonkeygate* in the Middle Ages this major shopping street no longer runs as far as Sankey from Market Gate. The earlier view of 1926 shows the conflict developing between a growing stream of heavy traffic and pedestrians, only resolved in the 1980s. Holy Trinity Church, built in 1760, with the distinctive town clock can be seen on the left. (Previous page: Sankey Street in 1905 and 2010.)

Sankey Street is pedestrianised

By the time of this photograph from the 1970s (above) the Warrington New Town Development Plan had already proposed the pedestranisation of Sankey Street. All the buildings to the right would be replaced with the new Golden Square. Woolworth's had been a familiar presence on the street since the 1920s but became one of the most high profile UK high street casualties of the economic recession of 2008, finally closing its doors in January 2009.

This wasn't just a street widening scheme....

Marks & Spencer arrived in Sankey Street in the 1930s. In anticipation of the imminent plans to widen the street and redevelop the Market Place it was designed with a temporary single storey frontage which soon became a permanent feature! Eventually pedestrianisation replaced road widening schemes and in 1977 a new Marks & Spencer's store opened in the first phase of Golden Square. In 1978 the original store and its neighbours were demolished.

Marking time at the corner of Bold Street and Sankey Street 1924 and 2009

Familiar local stores such as Broadbent and Turner and Eustance the jeweller have relocated; T. J. Hughes has replaced the Co-operative Store. New modern architecture swept away the Victorian; notably the elaborate Woolpack Inn on the corner of Bold Street (behind Eustance's clock) creating a featureless 1970s block or the mellow brickwork of Golden Square (left.) Brash shop signage and street furniture dominate the modern scene.

How quickly Golborne Street changed!

Pedestrianisation of Sankey Street was made possibly by the construction of a new inner ring road (1970s-80s) which diverted traffic via Golborne Street, across Horsemarket Street, Scotland Road and Academy Way to Bridge Foot. A monolithic multi storey car park was created in neighbouring Legh Street and a bus station off Golborne Street (see 2004 image below.) By 2007 the Golden Square extension turned Golborne Street into a traffic free Hilden Platz!

Hunting the White Hart in Sankey Street

The section of Sankey Street between Golborne Street and Legh Street was widened in 1928 in an ambitious scheme to create a dual carriageway; with new civic buildings and shopping centre. Riley, the game dealer, Browne's the hairdresser, the white-painted old White Hart and the posh Winmarleigh café had to give way to William and Segar Owens' impressive new block. All to no avail as the Second World War ended the dream.

Sankey Street looking towards Market Gate/Golden Square

These two views dramatically illustrate the potential impact of turning Sankey Street into a dual carriageway! Perhaps the thought was enough to send the man in the bowler hat scurrying into the old White Hart (near left above) for a reviving drink in 1926? Horobin's newsagents (top right) with its stone flagged floors survived to the early twenty-first century in a block dating back to at least the early 1800s.

Sankey Street at the junction with Springfield Street 1920s and 2010

This relatively tranquil part of Sankey Street still has a tale to tell. To the right ,on the corner of Springfield Street, was a cinema; firstly the ornate Picturedrome (above) and by the 1950s the Cameo. On the left of the 2010 view is a remodelled eighteenth century Bank House, once home to William Allcard, a Victorian railway engineer who worked with Stephenson on the Liverpool to Manchester railway.

Changing the guard between Springfield Street and Winmarleigh Street

The troops had a grandstand view for the visit of King Edward VII and Queen Alexandra in July 1909 but they had a long wait for the motorcade to arrive at the Town Hall, before leaving a bare four minutes later! The impressive Warrington Guardian building graced the street from the early 1880s to the modernisation of 1973. The newspaper relocated to the modernised Academy building at Bridge Foot in 1987.

Something's missing from the Town Hall Lawn!

Today Sankey Street has two historic landmarks, the Town Hall and the Golden Gates. Once there was a third: the Walker Fountain (above *c.* 1940). This ornate cast iron fountain was presented to Warrington in May 1900 in memory of Peter Walker of Walker's brewery. Manufactured by McFarlane and Company of Glasgow it dominated the site and drenched passers by before being demolished for scrap metal in a patriotic wartime gesture in March 1942!

All change opposite the Town Hall 1970-2010

Warrington's Town Hall is a classical eighteenth century building by acclaimed architect James Gibbs. Facing it today across Sankey Street are two starkly modern glass and concrete office blocks and Salem Baptist chapel, all built in the early 1970s. The earlier photograph shows the towering Conservative Club which together with the Warrington Guardian offices once formed part of the business empire of the Greenall brewery dynasty.

CHAPTER 5
Horsemarket Street

Horsemarket Street viewed from Market Gate early twentieth and twenty-first centuries
Horsemarket Street was partially widened in the 1930s by the rebuilding of the shops on the right hand side, adjoining Buttermarket Street. Whilst Brigg and Company's shop on the corner opposite Turner's hosiery business was demolished in 1928 the rest of left hand side of the street survived into the late twentieth century. Today the Guardians look down on a broad vista to Central Station.

Recent developments in Horsemarket Street 1970s -2001

Fashion Fayre's trendy boutique signalled the closing days of old Horsemarket Street in the late 1970s (above) prior to the building of Golden Square. The town marked the new millennium with public art to enhance the newly pedestrianised areas. Most dramatic (and controversial) of these was the Well of Light with its ten Guardians of the town's heritage created by American artist Howard Ben Tre from materials inspired by the Warrington's industrial history.

Boldly going into the future along Horsemarket Street

Away from Market Gate there have also been several recent dramatic changes to the landscape of Horsemarket Street. The 1970s photograph above shows the premises at its junction with Queen Street and Bewsey Street which were demolished during the construction of the inner ring road in the 1970s. In 2006 a second major upheaval saw the striking new Warrington Interchange materialise there to replace the 1979 bus station.

Warrington's changing skyline 1980s and 2009

This bird's eye view over Horsemarket Street records the pace of change in this area of the town. The early 1980s view (above) shows Cockhedge Mill and its chimneys on the skyline next to the Parish Church spire with the new inner ring road to the right. By 2009 the mill has been replaced by a shopping complex; the spire reigns supreme and the proximity of the transport interchange and Central Station is clear.

Horsemarket Street looking towards Winwick Street 1900s and 2009

Where Horsemarket Street widens into Winwick Street at Central Station was where the actual horse market took place until 1911. The earlier view shows a livelier scene with reductions on prams at Pendlebury & Company's extensive shop on the left.

CHAPTER 6

Buttermarket Street

Buttermarket Street takes shape 1915-1970

The junction of Buttemarket Street and Bridge Street was the second portion of the Market Gate circus to be constructed in 1913-15. The earlier photograph (above) reveals how the street was widened and also the contrasting architectural style to the opposite corner shown on the 1970s photograph (below). Look on the previous page to see how the site changed by 1991 and after the arrival of the Guardians.

Buttermarket Street is pedestrianised

Warrington seemed a drabber place in the 1970s (above) and even supermarkets were smaller! A group stands outside the new Tesco store which was crammed into the building second from left. The new millennium brought a brighter outlook to the street with the creation of the Commons and the lavender gardens whilst Tesco relocated to a hypermarket on the site of the old Tetley Walker's brewery in Winwick Road.

Buttermarket Street meets Academy Street/Way 1978 and 2010

Buttermarket Street was also altered by the creation of a section of the inner ring road called Academy Way in the 1970s. Buildings on either side of its junction with Academy Street were demolished, including the Salvation Army citadel (top left.)

The changing face of Scotland Road and Cockhedge 2010 and early 1980s
In the 1980s town planning favoured relocating heavy industry away from a town centre and at the same time the retail sector was booming and looking for prime sites. The Cockhedge cotton mill had ceased to be viable and Peter Stubs File making works (seen below centre) had relocated. Charterhall properties stepped in to develop the Cockhedge shopping centre opened in 1984.

Looking along Buttermarket Street to Market Gate from Scotland Road

It was a long and winding road along Buttermarket Street in the 1900s and hard to recognise from the steps of New Town house today. The buildings on the left hand side of the street were replaced in the 1930s. The old premises on the corner of Scotland Road, next to Chorley's shop, (right) were first redeveloped as the Odeon Cinema (1937-1994) and later as a public house.

A century of change in Lower Buttermarket Street

Today the vast concrete edifice of New Town House dominates Lower Buttermaket Street between Scotland Road and Orford Street. The lively scene at Walking Day in 1906 shows a concentration of smaller shops. Thomas Sudlow the tobacconist and estate agent had Walter Dumbell the hairdresser and Gallop's herbalist as his immediate neighbours. Next was a boot dealer, newsagent, general dealer, wholesale bedstead manufacturer, plumber, butcher, draper and other assorted shop keepers.

The junction of Mersey Street and Church Street 1905 and 2010

At its southern end Buttermarket Street reaches a junction with Mersey Street (right) and today continues into Church Street across a busy roundabout where few pedestrians venture. Three small boys could lean casually on a lamppost in 1905 (above) with only a tram and horse and cart passing leisurely by. Headlines proclaiming *"Another Russian defeat"* on the hoardings outside Downs's newsagent shop date this postcard to 1905.

Church Street looking towards the town centre 1911 and 2010

At the time of this Walking Day parade in 1911 Church Street was still at the heart of a community at Howley with works, shops and terraced houses, mostly dating from the nineteenth century. Until the development of Bridge Street from the thirteenth century Church Street was the town's main thoroughfare and site of the open market linked to a route to the old river crossing at Latchford.

Church Street looking towards Manchester Road

When local photographer Tonge produced his sepia postcard of Church Street in 1906 many locals probably felt it captured the sulphur fumes coming from Lockers, Rylands or the Firth wireworks nearby! The black and white seventeenth century building in the foreground (right) known as the Marquis of Granby pub was the headquarters of the Earl of Derby who had garrisoned the town as a stronghold for Charles I in the North West in 1642-3.

From wireworks to supermarket

How many shoppers pushing trolleys around Sainsbury's supermarket today realise that they could once have been made from wire produced on the site? Rylands wireworks arrived in Church Street about 1810 and within a century had become major employers exporting their products worldwide. A fleet of delivery lorries poses outside their impressive office block which together with the works was demolished in the early 1980s following a nationwide rationalisation of heavy industries.

WARRINGTON CHURCH, LANCASHIRE.

Warrington's Parish Church towers above Church Street

St Elphin's church, mentioned in the Domesday Book of 1086, originated by the Lord of the Manor's castle at Mote Hill and close to the ford over the Mersey. The picturesque 1830s scene above was deceptive: the medieval stone fabric was unsound, as newly appointed rector William Quekett discovered in 1854. He set about extensive rebuilding in 1859, culminating in the erection of the third highest parish church spire in England.

CHAPTER 7

Around the Town

LANE ENDS WINWICK

Lane ends at Winwick 1905

Weary travellers northward bound from Warrington would reach their first major landmark at Winwick Church. Dedicated to St. Oswald, who was killed at the Battle of Maserfelth in 642, the church dates from the earliest period of Christianity in the north-west. Passengers on the local horsebus might refresh themselves at the Swan (previous page) whilst poorer pedestrians could drink at the fountain erected in memory of John Thompson, a highway surveyor.

A Lovely Lane to Bewsey

By the thirteenth century the Boteler family, Lords of the Manor of Warrington, had chosen to settle in this *"beau see"* or beautiful place, still remote from the town. By the mid seventeenth century Bewsey Hall was no longer at the heart of local government. Nineteenth century railways brought heavy industry encroaching on Lovely Lane's picturesque cottages (above.) In July 1927 Warrington's first major estate of council housing opened at *"Bewsey Garden Suburbs."*

From Silver Screen to washing windscreens in Orford Lane

Long before the days of television, DVDs, the internet and the family car Warringtonians found their entertainment at the movies . The Queens Cinema was just one of the local picture palaces where people could escape from the reality of daily life. Changing fashions saw cinemas all over the country demolished in the later twentieth century and the Orford Lane site became first a garage and later a car wash.

The changing face of the corner shop in Orford Lane

Located on the corner of Leonard Street and Orford Lane, Melia's (pictured above
c. 1900) was a typical "Family grocers", with personal service from the manager and his
white-aproned assistant and an errand lad on hand for home deliveries. In the 1980s
Warringtonians abandoned the corner shop for the supermarket and Melia's became a
launderette. By 2010 another corner shop appeared in Orford Lane serving the area's
diverse community.

Green Street divided as the car is king of the road

Green Street Bank Quay was typical of many Warrington communities in 1900. Side by side with the terraced houses were all the shops the housewife would need each day before the age of the fridge-freezer. The late twentieth century brought the convenience of weekly supermarket shopping but the car which made this possible saw Green Street bisected by improvements to the local road network to relieve traffic congestion.

All change at Sankey Bridges?

In April 1902 the first Latchford bound tram departed from Sankey Bridges along the old Liverpool Road and past the Black Horse Inn (inset.) This half timbered building was no stranger to history. In 1643 it took centre stage in one of the skirmishes in the English Civil War. On 5 April Sir William Brereton, Captain Edward Sankey and Parliamentary troops advanced on Warrington, capturing the building, then a royalist stronghold owned by Edward Bridgman.

Knutsford Road looking towards Bridge Foot

Once the Number 1 tram passed through the town centre it made its way across Warrington Bridge and down Knutsford Road to Latchford. The tram lines and poles carrying the electric current are clearly visible on the early 1900s photograph (above.) Today Knutsford Road is much wider; most of the terraced houses and the Old Pin Factory (top right) are long gone.

An urban idyll at Latchford Weir

Early eighteenth century improvements to the Mersey helped establish Warrington as an industrial centre but led to the disappearance of the ancient river crossing at Latchford. The 1721 Mersey & Irwell Navigation Act allowed promoters to build locks, tow paths, small canals and weirs to control the river flow. Outwardly the scene at Latchford Weir seems little changed since the 1860s view above but notice the changes to the Parish Church in the background.

The Plague House was there in black and white!
In the background of this 1920s Latchford Walking Day procession (above) is the notorious "Plague House" built for Richard Warburton in 1656. Tradition states that several of its occupants were struck down by the deadly outbreaks of the contagious disease which led up to the Great Plague of 1666. The nineteenth century discovery of hastily buried human remains in the garden help confirm the story. Today only the garden wall survives.

Latchford's Walking Day procession gives way to a parade of shops

The tram linked Latchford with the town centre in the 1900s and encouraged white collar workers to move to the neat bay-windowed superior terraced housing along Knutsford Road. This Edwardian Walking Day procession (above) still has the air of a village celebration but by the mid twentieth century shops had replaced houses in the village centre as semis in leafier Stockton Heath and Grappenhall seemed even more desirable.

The impact of the Manchester Ship Canal

Between 1890 and 1894 the cutting of the Manchester Ship Canal (popularly known as *The Big Ditch)* had a dramatic impact on the landscape of South Warrington. Latchford was cut off from Thelwall and Grappenhall; Wilderspool isolated from Stockton Heath and mainly reliant on the swing bridges. Birtles dramatic photograph (above) shows the scale of the construction work, with the high level railway bridge and Latchford Locks in the background.

A brave new world arrives at Latchford Locks

In 1906 Richmond's relocated their foundry to a site by Latchford Locks (above) becoming a major employer. The site had a large foundry and enamelling department, grinding, sand blasting, machine, assembling, tin smiths' and Gas fire radiant making shops, water heating department, warehouses and of course produced the famous *New World* Cookers. By 2010 Richmond's had vanished to be replaced by a new housing development of Edgewater Park.

Last orders at Greenalls

By 1791 the Greenall brewing dynasty was already well established at Wilderspool headed by St. Helens brewer Thomas Greenall who had seen a business opportunity at the existing Saracens Head site. Good supplies of pure well water, together with ample quantities of locally grown grain for malting, a good transport network and wealthy investors made Warrington an ideal choice for expansion. Rivals like Walker's (later Tetley Walker) and Burtonwood Ales followed but Greenall's integrated into local public life, becoming not only major employers but also in Sir Gilbert Greenall's case the town's MP with a fine residence at Walton Hall. By the early 1900s the Wilderspool brewery had been completely rebuilt and soon had a fleet of Sentinel steam lorries (seen above) to deliver to the firm's regional chain of pubs. Brewing ended at Wilderspool in 1991 and the site was subsequently redeveloped as offices.

Workhorses and pleasure craft at London Bridge Stockton Heath

Today colourful canal craft moor at London Bridge but until the mid nineteenth century the Bridgewater canal was still an important part of the regional transport network. Local artist Oswald Garside captured the atmospheric scene below in the 1930s, possibly intended to use the horse drawn working barge as a subject for one of his acclaimed paintings.

Stockton Heath becomes commuter belt 1904

In 1902 Warrington's new tram network reached as far as Wilderspool leaving Stockton Heath residents using the local horse bus or walking over the swing bridge. The photograph (above) shows workman laying the tracks which would finally link the village with the town centre. Many of Warrington's middle class began the commute from the suburbs to their offices with an increasing volume of traffic clogging up Stockton Heath as the car became king.

Victoria Square Stockton Heath in 1907 and 2010

Victoria Square is the heart of Stockton Heath so it was the natural choice for General Buller to plant a commemorative tree on his visit to Warrington in February 1907 (see page 96.) Despite the cold a crowd assembled near the Mulberry Tree and the *"main streets of the village were in holiday garb, flags and bunting fluttering gaily in the breeze."* Eventually the tree was discreetly moved as it impeded traffic!

Picture postcard Grappenhall

Gropenhale (Grappenhall) was recorded in the Domesday Book of 1086 and this ancient parish once included Latchford. St. Wilfrid's Church retains the village's medieval history with its effigy of a Norman knight and ancient stained glass. Even the coming of the nearby Bridgewater Canal failed to disturb its tranquillity although some of its quaint thatched cottages still in evidence in the 1900s (above) have given way to more solid stone buildings.

Appleton Thorn 1900s and twenty-first century

Appleton with a number of neighbouring areas of south Warrington became part of the borough at local government reorganisation in 1974. The village's unique tradition, the "Bawming of the Thorn," takes place on or about St. Peter's Day (29 June) each year. Local children decorate or "bawm" the village's thorn tree as a reminder of the original planted in medieval times by the lord of the manor from a sprig of the Glastonbury Thorn.

THELWALL VILLAGE

Time seems to standstill in Thelwall

It seems that all the village children had come to pose for this 1900s postcard view (above) of Thelwall village! Today the Pickering Arms (right) still recalls the legend that *"In the year 923 King Edward the Elder founded a city here and called it Thelwall."* The fortified site may have long disappeared but Thelwall viaduct has assured that its name is not forgotten.

Leisure time at Lymm Dam

These Edwardian residents of Lymm might never have heard of global warming but they were certainly not skating on thin ice! Even then Lymm Dam was a popular leisure spot but it is a man made landscape. When improvements were made to the Warrington, Altrincham and Stockport turnpike road in 1821-4 the opportunity was taken to include a reservoir to supply local industries such as the corn and slitting mills. Rising above the dam is St. Mary's Church which has medieval origins. In 1850 famous Newcastle architect John Dobson was commissioned to rebuild it, although the fifteenth century tower had to be replaced in 1887. Although Lymm's industries have gone the dam remains a well loved resource today, especially with anglers.

Spot the difference in Lymm 1900s and 2010

Although Lymm Cross (seen opposite) may be Lymm's most familiar landmark the Millstone Hotel (above) was once an equally familiar site. The two large buildings which once hung over the lower dam housed shops and a tea room have since been demolished to expose the white cottages of the Groves.

CHAPTER 8

Caught on Camera

Walking Day pomp 1895 and 2010

Friday 28 June 1895 saw a double celebration in Warrington. Firstly it was the town's unique Walking Day which was begun in 1834 by Rector Horace Powys as a counter-attraction to the drunkenness and gambling of Newton races. Secondly Councillor Frederick Monks of Monks Hall Iron Foundry presented the magnificent gates to the town. Originally designed for Sandringham House they were adapted with Warrington's Coat of Arms and later gilded to their intended design.

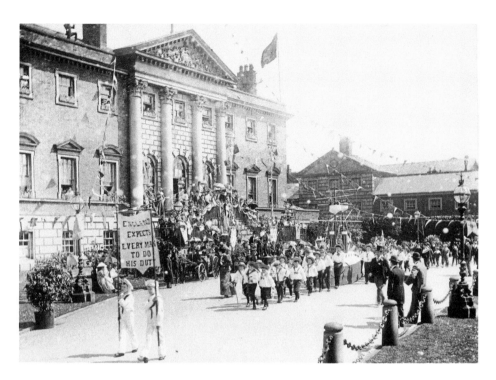

Let the procession begin!

Today's procession begins through the Town Hall Gates but originally the Mayor watched from the Town Hall balcony. The 1897 Jubilee Walking Day (below) celebrated the sixtieth anniversary of Victoria's accession to the throne. St James's Sunday School, Latchford, adopted a patriotic theme. The Warrington Guardian reported that, *"A number of lads dressed as sailors drew a model of an ironclad whilst two lads in front carried a banner containing Nelson's last signal to the fleet.*

Travelling Through Time at Warrington Museum

Founded in 1848 Warrington Museum was the third local authority museum to be created in the country and the first in the North West of England. By 1853 the museum and its associated library had outgrown its rented premises in Friars Gate and the search began for a new home. Thanks to the generosity of local landowner Mr Wilson Patten a site was found off Bold Street. Plans for an ambitious building were commissioned from leading architect John Dobson, and then rejected because of their cost. A more affordable option from Mr. Stone of Newton le Willows was accepted and work could finally begin on building which its supporters referred to as a *"Home for the Muses,"* to make art, literature and science accessible to all. The three storey building would include galleries; reading room, library and space for the School of Art. The Foundation Stone was laid on 22 September 1855 by William Beamont who buried a time capsule under the stone. The occasion was documented by Samuel Mather Webster, one of the town's earliest photographers. His remarkable photograph (above) illustrates the contemporary description by the Warrington Guardian's reporter: *" Leaving the procession to wend its way ...by way of Horsemarket Street, Bridge Street and the Arpley Station ..we found a crowd of at least 2,000 persons around the site after 12 o'clock. On the site itself a platform had been erected for those engaged in the ceremony and opposite to it several rows of benches filled with elegantly dressed ladies."* In 2007 Warrington Museum celebrated the 150th anniversary of the opening of the Victorian building with a much less formal occasion where over 3,000 people welcomed time traveller Dr Who and his adversaries, the Daleks!

Warrington makes the news!

Occasionally Warrington finds itself at the forefront of national news stories and fortunately local photographers have recorded the events for posterity. Liberal leader William Ewart Gladstone was the first major politician to begin the custom of barnstorming tours of the country during election campaigns; a concept taken for granted today. He twice halted at Bank Quay station to address enthusiastic crowds of supporters from his railway carriage, even though his December 1879 visit was on a dark, freezing foggy evening. The pioneering and rare photograph (above left) by J. E. Birtles is more likely to have been taken early on a morning in November 1885 when his train paused in a railway siding en route to Scotland. Liberal Democrat leader Nick Clegg's visit on Friday 16 April 2010 saw a media scrum of press and television crews crowd around the unexpected star of the first national televised TV election debate as his battle bus halted at the Haliwell Jones stadium, next to Tesco's supermarket! Pictures of the event were quickly broadcast around the world by satellite and the Warrington Guardian's readers could almost instantly see their photographer's work (above right) on the paper's website.

For the Fallen; Warrington's memorial to its Boer War heroes

In 2010 Warringtonians worry about loved ones serving in Afghanistan but in February 1907 it was time to remember members of the South Lancashire regiment killed in the recent Boer War against South Africa. An expectant crowd arrived in Queens Gardens to witness General Sir Redvers Buller unveil the memorial on a day when *"the sun shone brightly and banners and streamers flew in the breeze."* After a civic reception at the Town Hall the ceremony began at 3 pm. Sculptor Alfred Drury invited the distinguished war hero to unveil the bronze statue which *"represented the late Colonel MacCarthy O'Leary as he appeared in the Battle of Pieters Hill where he fell directing his troops."* Commemorative plaques also record all the men of the regiment killed in the South African campaign and a list of the engagements they fought.

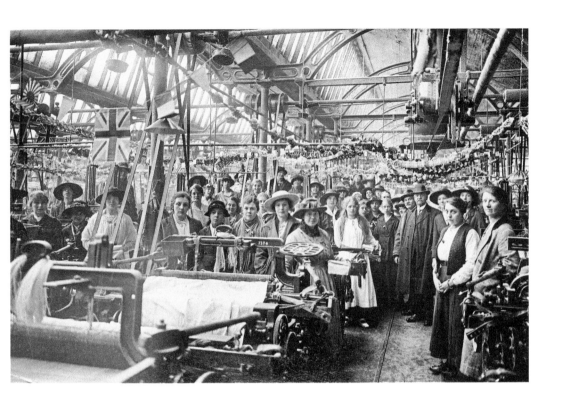

The clatter of the looms are silenced at Cockhedge

Warrington was never dependent on the cotton trade unlike neighbouring mill towns and eventually only Armitage & Rigby's Cockhedge Mill remained. During the First World War the firm was criticised for not supplying the expected quota of recruits. But the majority of the workforce was female, apart from the male fitters who kept the machinery running and the foremen. The spinners and weavers did their patriotic duty despite this producing khaki cloth for the troops. The mill girls waited anxiously to hear the news of the Armistice on 11 November 1918 and the news that peace had been declared. Two days later the looms fell silent and 4,000 people queued to admire the red, white and blue decorations in the mill, contributing to a collection for war veterans. Today only the salvaged roof girders remain in the Cockhedge shopping centre.

The camera *sometimes* lies!

The arch at Bruche Bridge (above) was only a transient feature set up to welcome King Edward VII and his consort on his short visit to Warrington in July 1909. In December 1977 Warringtonians arrived at Market Gate to discover that it had suddenly become part of Moscow! Cartoonist Bill Tidy had created a sixty foot mural of Red Square complete with Russian soldiers. Fortunately it was merely an advertising campaign for Greenall's Vladivar whisky.

Road works: every photographer's nightmare?

The unknown photographer who recorded the installation of electric cabling in Lymm in the 1920s probably set out to record this momentous event. In 2009-10 it was hard to avoid the disruption to streetscapes caused by remedial work to local sewerage schemes. Future historians will doubtless remark on the greater attention paid to health and safety in the twenty-first century!

Biotechnology: Warrington's new manufacturing industry for the twenty-first century

Acknowledgements

This volume has mainly been compiled from the extensive photographic collections of Warrington Museum and the Library's Local History Archive.

The picture of Nick Clegg on Page 91 appears courtesy of the *Warrington Guardian* newspaper.

Acknowledgements are also due to all those who have contributed to the photographic archive and added to our knowledge of Warrington. Particular thanks are owing to all the professional and amateur photographers who have documented the changing face of the town. Every effort has been made to trace the copyright holders but the Museum is always interested to learn further details of any of the featured images.